# Wings
## of
# Faith

**By Josephine Cunnington Edwards**

*Illustrated by Jim Padgett*

**TEACH Services, Inc.**
P U B L I S H I N G
www.TEACHServices.com • (800) 367-1844

Copyright © 2023 Josephine Cunnington Edwards
Copyright © 2023 TEACH Services, Inc.
ISBN-13: 978-1-4796-1454-7 (Paperback)
ISBN-13: 978-1-4796-1455-4 (ePub)
Library of Congress Control Number: 2022943208

All Scriptures, unless otherwise stated, are taken from the New King James Version®.
Copyright © 1982 by Thomas Nelson. Used by permission. All rights reserved.

Originally published by Southern Publishing Association © 1964

Published by

**TEACH Services, Inc.**
P U B L I S H I N G
www.TEACHServices.com • (800) 367-1844

# Table of Contents

Strange Object on the Ceiling. . . . . . . . . . . . . . . . . . . . . . . . . . . . . . . . .5

Raise in Pay. . . . . . . . . . . . . . . . . . . . . . . . . . . . . . . . . . . . . . . . . . . . .13

Rich—and Poor Again. . . . . . . . . . . . . . . . . . . . . . . . . . . . . . . . . . . . .17

How Lem Found the Money. . . . . . . . . . . . . . . . . . . . . . . . . . . . . . . . .23

On His Own Now. . . . . . . . . . . . . . . . . . . . . . . . . . . . . . . . . . . . . . . . .27

Em Finds a Job. . . . . . . . . . . . . . . . . . . . . . . . . . . . . . . . . . . . . . . . . . .33

In With the Wrong Crowd. . . . . . . . . . . . . . . . . . . . . . . . . . . . . . . . . . .37

Great Changes . . . . . . . . . . . . . . . . . . . . . . . . . . . . . . . . . . . . . . . . . . .43

Sickness in the Night . . . . . . . . . . . . . . . . . . . . . . . . . . . . . . . . . . . . . .49

Faith Takes Wings. . . . . . . . . . . . . . . . . . . . . . . . . . . . . . . . . . . . . . . .53

# Strange Object on the Ceiling

T HE GRASS grows thick and green on Calvin's grave. The stone has nestled down now among the roses as if at long last it is content to stay there. Nearly half a century has come and gone since the long, horse-drawn procession brought him there and put him away. Oh, it was a crying shame! Calvin was such a merry boy, always laughing and swinging his arms about or sprinting forward as he played. His muscles were firm and his eyes clear blue. When he laughed, it was so infectious that you felt yourself grin too—even though you hadn't heard the joke.

When you bend over and push aside a little curtain of ivy and rub away the moss from the bottom, you can read:

"CALVIN EDWARD McRAE
1898—1914
Gone to his rest"

Then, if you had known him, you'd feel as if that little headstone felt disgraced, for its face is covered with five-fingered ivy leaves in very shame. And you would feel again that aching void that Calvin's going meant to all of his friends. And you would try and try to understand why.

Some twenty-four years ago a man knelt by that grave and pulled aside the ivy leaves. His name was Emerson Chadwick, and he sighed as he read the lettering. "Calvin Edward McRae. I'll never forget him. Best boy that ever drew a breath. Just as jolly and good a fellow as I ever did see. We were pals, he and I. You'd never believe there was ten years' difference in our ages. He liked to putter around with me in my workshop. Always making gliders like the ones Orville Wright used to make back in Dayton.

" 'Mr. Chadwick,' I remember he used to say, 'airships will be thicker than flies before long.' I laughed at him then, but he was right. He never lived to see it, though. Oh, it was a shame he had to get shot like that. He'd have made a minister, a missionary, or a college president! And yet, and yet—if he hadn't died— where would I be? Where would I be?"

The thought so struck Em Chadwick that he looked up and blinked hard to keep back the tears that brimmed his eyes. What a sad life he had lived—till Calvin had come along. His mind went back over the past fifty years, and he forgot he was kneeling by the grave.

***

The milk slopped out a little on Em's skinny legs, for the tin pail jogged as he swung it on its wobbly bail and gaped at things when he passed Orville and Wilbur Wright's bicycle shop. There were all kinds of things there that interested little boys. Em liked especially to see the bicycle with the tall front wheel and the tiny back wheel.

One day he observed a strange-looking object hanging from the ceiling, made from strips of bamboo, sheets of heavy paper, and bits of cork and hard wood. Rubber bands were stretched across it from one point to another. "What's that?" he inquired of someone near. The milk pail was set down and Em's pudgy, dirty finger pointed at the fragile contraption.

The mechanic laughed as he bent over a bicycle part he was cleaning. Then, good-naturedly, he laid it aside, wiped his hands on some waste, and took the curious-looking object down and began to wind up the rubber bands.

"This is a helicopter," he said. "It'll fly like a bird. Don't tell, but Wilbur and I are talking of building one sometime that a man can fly in. You see if we don't, for we're working and studying too!" The young man released the little ship, and it flew gracefully up, then glided down as the rubber bands unwound themselves.

"You couldn't do that!" scoffed the boy. "Nobody can fly, except angels and birds and flies—and kites. Better stick to bikes. They're the best invention anybody ever could make."

> *"Listen, fellow," he said, "the woods are full of things that have never yet been invented or thought of."*

Then little Em Chadwick saw a change come over the face of the young mechanic. His eyes grew dark and thoughtful, and he looked down at him for a long time.

"Listen, fellow," he said, "the woods are full of things that have never yet been invented or thought of; why, there are possibilities for development of even the gas buggy till nearly everyone will have one. And mark my word, airships will be as thick someday as those birds." And he pointed to a big flock of sparrows that flew up from the trash in the gutter.

Little Em picked up the helicopter and examined it with little-boy curiosity. He wondered whether he would ever fly in one of those things. He thought not. Why, if he so much as got up in Ramsey's barn loft, he got

*The milk slopped out a little on Em's skinny legs.*

dizzier than scat. No. Orville Wright was a smart fellow, but he was wrong. Nobody would ever be crazy enough to go up in an airship.

After pondering the matter for a while, he remembered the milk. He must deliver it and get home. He picked up his bucket and started to wind his way around piles of bicycle parts to the door of the shop. He ran at a fast dogtrot up the sidewalk toward the Wright house. It was only a matter of minutes till he had the milk at the door of the big, clean kitchen.

He found time, later in the day, to go back to the bike shop to see Orv. He had shown him the helicopter. He had been patient. Maybe he'd talk to a fellow. And he knew all about mechanical things. Maybe he could learn something. Emerson went in the shop. He found Orv busy reassembling a bicycle. He was friendly and willing to hear him and looked full at the lad with clear, intelligent eyes.

"Why, Em, we aren't the first ones who ever thought of flying. Not by a jugful. Nearly seven hundred years ago a very wise man in England named Roger Bacon wrote about it. What he said was so interesting to me that I learned it by heart. It went something like this:

> Machines for navigating are possible without rowers, so that great ships suited to rivers and oceans, guided by one man, may be borne with greater speed than if they were full of men. Likewise cars may be made so that without a draught animal they may be moved with inestimable speed. And flying machines are possible, so that a man can sit in the middle and turn some device by which artificial wings may beat the air in the manner of a flying bird.

"Listen, Em, I'll tell you a secret. I believe we are really going to make a machine that flies. You'll see. Haven't you ever read about Otto Lilienthal?"

Orville went over to the wall and took down a faded newspaper clipping.

"Otto Lilienthal," he said soberly, "was a smart German fellow who worked for years on man-carrying kites. He rode in them himself, but about three years ago an accident happened. His big kite stalled fifty-five feet from the ground, and Lilienthal was killed. I'll tell you, boy, the world lost a great man. Ever since my brother and I read about it, we have been trying to make a contraption that will fly. We think it would be great sport to zoom around high over the cities and towns in one.

"Mark my words," the young man continued, "men are going to learn everything they can about flight in the air, and what it is that keeps things in the air. If clever men can learn that, then they can avoid the thing that happened to Lilienthal. And you just see. There'll be flying machines yet!"

*** 

It was a wonder that little Emerson was interested in anything. When his parents had both died of typhoid fever, he was only a very small boy. A man and his wife—Lem and Sade Smith, distant cousins of Em's—came to take care of the child. They were lazy and slovenly and immediately began to be mean to poor little Emerson. Food was scarce. His clothing was ragged. The move was made before Em was old enough to fend for himself. He could faintly recall some of the lovely things his mother and father used to do for him. But they were all dim and uncertain now, and he could remember them only vaguely, with a desperate ache in his heart.

> *Hardship had its bearing on the character of the child. Because Lem and Sade were dirty and trashy, he determined not to be.*

He lived a lonely life. The cousins were ignorant and selfish. One wonders what his lovely, dainty mother would have said if she had known the cruel lot that had come to her little boy. But she did not know. Mercifully, she did not know.

Hardship had its bearing on the character of the child. Because Lem and Sade were dirty and trashy, he determined not to be. He hated liquor and tobacco because Lem and Sade indulged in them so freely.

But time will pass—even if life isn't too happy. Em Chadwick had just passed not only a lean and stark winter but his eleventh birthday as well. His face was a little more pointed and his arms a little skinnier. On this particular spring day he was leaving the house when a gang of the neighbor boys called to him.

"C'mon, Em. Play us a game of marbles!" they shouted. They had scratched a circle in the pavement dust and there had deposited their choice glassies, chinies, agates, and ironies.

"Bring your bag of pedads and play us a game, Em," bawled a black-eyed urchin in a huge stretched-out turtle-neck sweater augmented by a pair of cutdown moleskin pants.

*Em stood on the cold street corner, trying to sell papers to the passing crowds.*

Em hitched up his trousers and shook his head.

"Can't do it," he answered. "I have to take this book back to a friend of mine. He lent it to me to study. He wanted it back because he's studying up on flying machines. It's a good book all right. It's named *Animal Mechanism,* and it's all about how birds fly. Someday there are going to be airships."

"Oh yeah?" scoffed a redheaded chap, as he squatted to direct his shooter skillfully into the circle of marbles. "Those Wright fellows who own a bike shop have gone crazy over airships."

A loud chorus of approving guffaws greeted the redhead's remark. Nothing could be more absurd to their young minds than airships in the sky!

"You fellows make me tired," Emerson said loftily. "There'll be flying machines yet, say what you want to. Maybe—maybe I'll even ride in one myself."

He stopped long enough to wither the little group of urchins again with a scornful, superior glance. Then he proceeded grandly up the street toward the bike shop.

# Raise in Pay

**L**EAVING the book, he went on uptown to the newspaper office and got his usual daily allotment of papers.

It was a discouraging task, this newspaper business of his. Lem had started him out in it two years before. He had had to stand hour after hour on the street corners in soggy shoes and inadequate clothes to earn a miserable pittance. Then as soon as he got home, the drunken man who was supposed to be taking care of him seized his money. Em dimly sensed the injustice, but what could he do? There was no one to tell, no one to care. He just had to go on and live and do as he had done, because there was nothing else to do.

The kerosene lamp flared up and smoked a sooty blob on the chimney when he opened the door to the kitchen. When he came home at night, something inside him always recoiled at the smells and sights and sounds that assailed him. But tonight he hugged a little secret to his ragged breast. Usually he was able to bring home fourteen or fifteen cents at the most all these cold, gloomy months. Lem would promptly confiscate the money, not even leaving him so much as a penny. Then when he complained at having to go out to sell the papers when the weather was stormy or bitter cold, he got a thrashing.

But today something good had happened—something entirely unlooked for. He had grown weary in his very soul of his regular corner. It was near the car stop, where everyone was in a hurry. No one seemed to notice a ragged little newsy with some damp papers clutched in his skinny hands. Muffled in warm woolens, intent on their own problems, they swept past him.

After an hour of standing soggy and shivering on that particular day, he wandered away from his usual place. Walking aimlessly down a side street, he came upon a regular gold mine. He wondered that no one had found it before. There was a row of bakeries and delicatessens, their bright show windows flooding the sidewalk. A grillwork in front of one of them breathed its huge, warm breath upon him, like a great panting, friendly animal. He stood over it gratefully and tried to still his chattering teeth. He was so engrossed by his own relief from discomfort that he was utterly amazed when two pennies were thrust into his hand and a newspaper was eased out of his satchel by a laughing passerby.

His salesmanship came to the surface spontaneously, and he began to really sell as customers came out of the hot bakeries with loaves of bread thrust under their arms and bags of cookies in their hands. Invariably they stopped and bought a paper from him. They had time for a kind word to say to the lad, too, and he needed that worse than he needed to sell papers.

In just a few minutes he was sold out. He tore around the corner to the newspaper office as fast as he could go and got another batch. They, too, were soon gone. Three times he had to go back.

There was another reason why it was good to be standing on that grating. The hot air that came through the ventilators smelled like hot bread and raisin pie and cinnamon rolls. It made his mouth water.

Soon a motherly woman with a gray fringed shawl over her head and laugh wrinkles around her eyes came out. She stopped and patted him on the head and asked him if he was cold. Opening a crackly paper bag, she selected two big cookies, full of fat, juicy raisins, and put them into his chapped hand. Nothing before that he remembered ever tasted so good.

After he counted his pennies, he found that instead of the usual fourteen or fifteen, he had sixty-eight. As he was putting the money into his wet pocket, he dropped part of it down the grating. It was discouraging to see those pennies that he had worked so hard for spread out four or five feet below him. Acting on an impulse, he entered the bakery and spoke to the smiling woman who presided over the counter.

"Say, lady, I dropped some of my newspaper money down your grating out in front. Is there any way I can get it out of there?"

Possibly the appealing look in the lad's eyes was irresistible, or perhaps the woman was naturally good-natured and felt particularly generous after such a good rush of trade. She opened a door at the back and beckoned.

"Scoot down those stairs and tell Gus. He's the baker. He can get them for you."

Em "scooted," and came into a bright, hot basement room. Great bowls as big as washtubs were full of spongy dough. Gus was just pulling a huge tray of cookies out of the oven when he spied Em.

"What now, fellow?" he queried in a loud, jolly voice.

Em told him his troubles. Gus waddled over, swung one of the windows easily on its hinges, and told the lad to crawl in and get his pennies.

When Emerson emerged with a handful of coppers, Gus was waiting for him.

"Don't want a little job of work tonight, do you, young fellow?" Big Gus detained the lad just as he was ready to scamper up the stairs. "My helper quit on me, and I've got lots of pie tins that need washing. I have so much work to do that I can't get at it myself. You look like a fellow that doesn't mind a job of work once in a while."

"Why, yes," answered Em, wonderingly thinking of the old proverb that says, "When it rains, it pours." "I wouldn't mind earning a little money on the side."

"Then take off your coat, and I'll give you an apron." The baker hung the ragged little jacket up beside his huge coat. Then he waddled over and puffingly reached up and took a big apron down from the high shelf. It was plain that it had been made for his own generous figure, for little Em was lost in it. But by hitches and knots it was made to stay on him. In five minutes he was working busily at the big sudsy tub with scrub brush and dish mop. In an hour the pans were all stacked, shining and clean, on cupboard shelves that Em took care to wash carefully first. Gus laid a silver quarter in his hand.

" 'Twould have taken a lazy fellow two hours. But you're a pert fellow. You made them shine better, too, than anyone I ever had. Come again tomorrow night and help me if you want to earn some more."

Em took out his old scuffed pocketbook and laid out fourteen cents to give Lem Smith when he got home. Seventy-nine cents he put into his purse. Now he could save for a bicycle. He had always wanted one. There was a good secondhand one for sale at Orville Wright's place for fifty-eight dollars. Bicycles were high in those early days. He'd sell papers by the bakeshop, and wash pie pans for Gus in the evening. He'd save money and get something for himself. There was a ray of hope ahead at last.

Gus good-naturedly scooped up a bag of broken cookies and thrust it into the boy's hands as he left. "There, fellow, is something for you to munch on. Looks like you need it. You look like the running gears of a cricket."

When Em reached home, Lem accepted the fourteen cents without a question. Em went quietly to his room, wondering how to hide the rest of the money so that Lem wouldn't take it from him.

# Rich—and Poor Again

THE POSITION in front of the bakery proved to be more than good luck for Em. It was at the beginning of a residential district, and the people grew to know and expect him. He got dozens of regular customers, while other newsies ran through the crowds in town, depending entirely on transients. The friendly woman in the bakery let him sell papers inside when it was raining or stormy. Then every evening he washed pie pans and bread tins for Gus. He even began to learn to draw pictures and do lettering, beautiful and shaded.

"You are such a smart fellow, I wish you were mine," said Gus affectionately one evening. Gus was an old bachelor, but he had grown very fond of the boy. Emerson learned that Gus had had a course in art in the country he had come from. And Gus learned that Em had lots of natural talent and a real bent toward drawing.

> *"You are such a smart fellow, I wish you were mine."*

On some of the long Sunday afternoons they were happy squaring off paper and making intricate patterns with curved and straight lines. Then they branched out into making the alphabet in Old English and other styles. The old Swiss got out a bottle of India ink, and Em was allowed to ink his own patterns and erase his pencilings.

This discovery of a talent gave Em more courage to face life. He lifted his chin and looked the whole world more squarely in the face. His voice took on an authoritative air, as if he were really something and somebody. He longed to have people respect him. He yearned for a worthwhile place in the world. Somehow he must achieve it.

He grew almost uncanny in the art of making money. He could almost smell out jobs. Then Gus threw many a chance in his way, too, taking an almost fatherly pride in the lad. It was a growing source of pride to Em that he was accumulating money. He was putting his little hoard in a flat tobacco can that Lem had emptied and discarded. He had hidden it away behind the dresser drawer in his room. Every night he added something to his store. He dropped the idea of buying a bicycle and determined to save till he was fifteen years old, and then do something big with his money— like buying a newsstand, where he could sell newspapers and magazines, candy bars, and small bags of almonds, walnuts, and pecans.

Emerson longed to be respected more than anything else in life. He wanted clean clothes—to be like the other boys. He wanted a home with clean windows, stiff curtains, smooth clean sheets. With that growing pile of money, he hoped to obtain them someday. Seeing the amount of money increasing, and knowing that soon he could buy the things he wanted so much, made him happy and able to bear the trials that came every day.

His cousin Sade shuffled about from morning till night in heelless slippers many sizes too large. She wore a shapeless gingham house dress, colorless and limp from unskillful laundering. Her hair was uncombed, and always she was complaining bitterly of severe pains in her stomach, her back, or her head. She would spend hours of every day reading cheap paperbacked novels.

Lem, her husband, was no better. Little Emerson never saw anyone drunk until he saw Lem deep "in his cups." It was a terrible experience for the lad. Then, too, Lem was lazy. Food was scarce and uncertain. Sade used to quarrel bitterly with him, but it did no good. Life was lean and hard for the boy.

Em was still quite young when he got his first job. He delivered milk for old man Courtes. It was on that route that he became acquainted with the Wright brothers. He delivered milk until the old man died and the cow was sold, but he never forgot the things he saw at the shop he had to pass every day. Here the two brothers who were one day to change the history of the world worked and experimented.

And now Emerson began to take courage. He was able to help himself. He saw that the only way out was for him to earn the way. There was no help for him but his two strong, young hands. He bent all of his energies to build himself a respectable life. Time went by fast because he was always busy.

As he grew older, he increased his allowance to Lemuel, so as to keep him from asking questions. Lemuel always took the money with a grunt and without a word of thanks, and trotted off to get his hat. Emerson's earnings kept Lem in beer and wine to drown his troubles. As soon as he could snatch the money from Emerson, he would slouch off down the street to the corner saloon, which handled his favorite brand of liquor.

\*\*\*

Em had found other things to engross him in his leisure hours. Experiments on gliders were going on all the time. The Wright brothers were actually coming to the correct notion of how to make machines stay in the air.

One night Wilbur Wright was sitting alone in his bicycle shop. Since there was nothing much to do, as business was quiet, the young man idly picked up an empty inner-tube box. It was oblong and made of cardboard, and reminded him of a biplane glider that a man named Chanute had made. Idly Wilbur twisted the box till the surface on one side sloped down and on the other side sloped up.

Looking at it, Wilbur suddenly had an idea. "Could not the surface of a glider be twisted in the same manner?" he wondered. "It would help to balance the machine in the air so that it wouldn't turn over." The young man leaped from his chair in excitement. In a moment he had the glue pot, and with trembling fingers he was constructing a model.

Em heard of the "wing warping," and wondered. He spent every moment he could spare from his various jobs listening to different mechanics talk of what was going on. He was on hand the day the Wright brothers departed for Kitty Hawk, North Carolina, where they were planning to build their gliders and make use of the constant mild wind that blows there. They carried a great deal of paraphernalia—boxes and bundles of materials, whole sheaves of plans and charts and statistics, besides their cases of tools.

Em wished he could go along. Dimly he sensed that their work was important and that he was witnessing history in the making. But he knew that he must not. That narrow can filled with tightly folded bills must be added to constantly. The last time he counted them there was more than two hundred dollars. Almost enough!

Old Jill Peebles had a "For Sale" sign out in front of her little newsstand. Em looked it over and haltingly asked her to name her price.

"More than you've got, kid," she had said coarsely and sarcastically. "First one that digs up a hundred dollars gets my newsstand. You see?"

"Yes, I see," replied Em slowly. "I've got it." Instantly the old woman became smooth as butter and began to show the serious sixteen-year-old her tiny quarters. They were dirty and slovenly. Already Em could see the place as he would transform it with white paint, linoleum, and white shelves. His other hundred dollars would make it into the cutest little store on the street.

"What's the rent?" he inquired.

"Ten dollars a month," replied the old woman.

Em wandered away. What was there to hinder him from setting up in business? He had quit school two years before. Of course, Mother would have wanted him to go on and get more education. But how could he? He couldn't buy himself as much as a shirt without Lem's becoming suspicious and asking where he got the money. But Mother was gone now, and everything she had stood for. Em's heart ached whenever he thought of her. Of course, Lem would try to get the money he earned in his stand, but Gus had promised to help him out, and testify for him before the courts if Lem made any trouble. A sudden decision to go ahead and buy the news-stand came over the boy.

Turning on his heel, he walked firmly home. Entering the house, he made his way to his bedroom. He shut and locked the door. Then carefully removing the bureau drawer, he laid it over on the sagging old bed. Reaching far in, he felt for the thin tin. He felt and felt, then filled with panic, he knelt down. Mumbling with fear and horror, he struck some matches and looked into the opening.

The money was gone!

*Lem waited greedily for Em to bring the money home each night.*

# How Lem Found the Money

LEM WAS a mixture of greed, vice, and laziness. He had earned only a very little money here and there since he had been turned out of his job for drunkenness and instability. He mended wagons and buggies and did odd jobs of repair work when he was sober. But that was all. The few cents that Emerson brought in kept him supplied with tobacco and liquor.

He waited every night restively for the boy's return. He hadn't a single suspicion for months —even years—that the boy was saving any money on the side. Em had increased the amount he gave him, and he was fairly satisfied. Emerson, at the age of sixteen, was earning as much as some grown men did in those days. Lem always pocketed Em's thirty, forty, or forty-five cents with a little grunt, which meant neither approval nor blame. He had the secret fear that if he showed any kind of gratitude to the boy, it might spoil him—might put ideas in his head.

But as Em shot up taller and his face began to look more and more like Alice, his mother, wicked old Lem became scared. Every time he looked at the boy furtively, he thought of the boy's gentle mother. He knew that she would disapprove of the way he had dealt with the lad, and he shuddered at the thought of Alice's accusing eyes, looking at him through the boy's. There was a lurking superstition in his cowardly old heart that a reckoning day was coming for him. But then he shook it off with a grunt and a growl and scolded the boy on every pretext. But the fear persisted.

> *He shuddered at the thought of Alice's accusing eyes, looking at him through the boy's. There was a lurking superstition in his cowardly old heart that a reckoning day was coming for him.*

One day it dawned on Lem's slow brain that Emerson was too happy. A boy who was treated as Emerson was couldn't be that happy unless something was wrong. He wasn't the same browbeaten, dodging little fellow he had been once. When Lem threatened to "hosswhip" him, the tall boy had smiled a little mysteriously and said not a word. Lem looked at Em's rippling young muscles and trembled at what the lad could do to him if he once lost his temper.

Then Lem's numbed brain tried to unravel the mystery. It was queer. He watched Emerson warily. He followed him stealthily one day down to his corner, where he sold the papers. Then he saw Em come out of the bakery slick and clean in decent clothes, selling papers right and left. Lem watched him for hours with hate and greed in his eyes. When the boy had sold out, he disappeared into the bakery. Lem slouched over and peered through the ventilator window to the basement. He heard the boy's voice ring out in laughter. Then by stooping over he got a glimpse of him. He was enveloped in a snowy apron and was doing something at a huge tub of dough. He could even hear the pops and thwacks as the boy pummeled and kneaded the elastic mass. He heard the rattle of pans, and big Gus making some sally, and the boy's clear, high laugh in answer.

Then, his mind filled with evil, covetous thoughts, tinged with suspicion, the man slouched off home. He'd track this thing down, he would. The boy had money. Of that he was sure. Now where was it?—that was the question. His eyes grew narrow, and he licked his thick lips greedily. He might not be able to get the best of Emerson with his fists, but he could outsmart him with his tricks. He was on the right track, he was sure.

He observed the lad narrowly. He noted that Em had changed to his ragged clothes when he came home that night. But he noticed how clean his hands and nails were when he handed him the usual half dollar. Then almost immediately the boy went upstairs to his room. Lem followed stealthily. He heard the click of the door button. Then stooping, puffingly, he gazed through the keyhole. Em was taking out the dresser drawer.

"Ha! So that's where!"

He heard the clink of a can. Then he slunk into a disorderly old closet, full of musty garments. A moment later the boy came out of his room and passed within a foot of him as he went downstairs.

Lem lost no time in getting the treasure. He slipped into the room and took out the drawer. Then, fumbling and pawing, he found the thin old tobacco tin, strangely heavy.

Laughing silently, he put it in his pocket and went to the kitchen to count it. First he made sure Em was gone. Sade was deep in a novel in the sitting room. Then he shoved back some coffee cups and some plates with grease and egg stains on them. He set the platter with a lone piece of limp meat expiring in a river of congealed grease on top of the bowl of cold gravy. He swiped the crumbs off the table onto the floor with his sleeve, and then poured the contents of the can onto the oilcloth.

Smoothing out creases in the tightly folded bills, he began to sort and to count.

Two hundred and thirty-seven dollars and forty-two cents! He counted it twice, puffingly and audibly, before he could believe it.

Lem leaned back in his chair and gasped. "Why, the selfish little kid!" he ejaculated. "He's been holding out on me."

# On His Own Now

**E**MERSON STOOD in his bedroom for a long time, trembling as he realized the importance of this new tragedy. And as he gazed at the empty drawer where the money had been, thoughts ran around in his troubled head like rats in a trap.

It came over him in a trice who had done it. Lem. That's who it was. He had never had anything Lem hadn't taken from him. That little can of money had meant much more to him than just so many dollar bills. It meant a real beginning of respectability. Then, when happiness had been within reach, it had been jerked away. It had been ever thus. Even as a little boy he would dream at night of Mother and fresh bread and clean linens. But when he was reveling in it, and basking in the sunlight of her smile, her sweet voice with its velvet cadences dwindled out into gray morning in Lem and Sade's

*His heart was broken in a thousand pieces. Life meant nothing now. Oh, what would he do?*

house. The dream ever recurred till it was almost a nightmare. And now it came over the trembling lad just how bleak his life had been.

His heart was broken in a thousand pieces. Life meant nothing now. Oh, what would he do? He leaned his throbbing forehead against the window. He was sick in his very soul. O Mother! Father! The boy's tortured soul cried out futilely to the loved ones who had been taken from him. And even the memory of them was dim and wavering.

Impetuously he pulled out his bureau drawers and began to gather together his few belongings. Sobs jerked at his throat. His eyes were scalded with tears he could not shed. Searching about, he found an old newspaper bag and crammed the ragged things into it. Opening his window, he stepped on the shed roof. "I'll go away," he thought. "Lem will never see me again."

He shinnied down the porch post and went off along the twilit street without so much as a backward glance. He walked around town for quite a while before he could formulate a plan.

Before long he went to the bakery. Gus wasn't there, but he got his good suit and things he had kept there, and left Gus a note. He hated to leave Gus worse than anything else. He made his way to the railroad station and waited there till night came down like a black curtain. A loud freight was pulling out, and Em slipped on and swung easily up the ladder. He crawled into the corner of an empty boxcar and sat huddled there shivering, partly from cold, partly from acute nervousness.

The train wheels with their regular rhythmic clatter seemed to be saying all kinds of things to him. His excited brain forced itself to form sentences that coordinated with the clatter. It tired him out, but he had to go on. For a long time the wheels spoke shrilly to him, as if even they were capable of scathing sarcasm: "Where's your money? Where's your money? Where's your money? Where's your money?"

Emerson nearly went crazy, until it seemed to change its tune: "No use crying. No use crying. No use crying. No use crying."

All through the long night he sat huddled there. Occasionally he felt the train slow up for a station, but he sat still, not even tempted to investigate. He was hungry and tired. He tried to relax for a little sleep, but the night was cool, and the stiff breeze sought out all the little rips and holes in his ragged garments. He took his newsbag and put it under his head. Curling up like a little animal hiding from some great beast, he at last fell into a restless slumber. He sobbed a little in his sleep, then turned over and slept soundly till morning streaked the sky.

When he awoke, he climbed up and peeked over the side of the boxcar. The train was going through beautiful country. There were gentle hills rising in the distance, and the whole countryside was crazy-patched with fields of grain and corn. He could see herds of cattle in the fields, cropping the lush grass, or drinking knee-deep in the dimpling streams. He felt the train slacken its speed and heard the whining of the brakes. A sudden resolve formed itself in his tired brain. He would get off here and wash in that clean little stream. Then he'd throw away these old clothes and put on the new ones he was carrying.

Suiting the action to the thought, he gathered up his belongings and prepared to descend. The train was moving very slowly when he jumped onto the gravel. He slid down the steep bank and found himself in a green field about forty or fifty feet from the gravel road.

He made his way to the little stream and washed as thoroughly as he could, using a clean pocket handkerchief for a washcloth. He changed his clothes behind a little growth of bushes. Then he shoved his old rags and tatters far in under the shadows of some rocks. They were badges of the life he was leaving forever, and he wanted to be rid of them. He was burning all bridges behind him.

He looked more like a real boy when he emerged. Corduroy trousers, a clean shirt, a corduroy coat, and a neat pair of black shoes. This had been the outfit he had worn to sell papers and work in the bakery. Gus had always sent his shirts and socks and handkerchiefs in with his own laundry. In this way the boy, innately fastidious, had achieved cleanliness.

Em felt better, but was ravenously hungry, as he swung along the road in his clean clothing. He was a handsome figure, his black hair parted and combed back smoothly and his cheeks red from his recent cold plunge. He could almost forget his money now in the joy of the new morning. Yet he had no idea where he was.

He had walked for perhaps an hour when he came upon a place that was clean and neat. The yards were cut smooth, and flowers bloomed around the house. On a big, white table near the kitchen door he could see the milk pans and buckets, washed clean, taking the sun. An old lady in a white cap and checkered gingham apron came out with a covered crock and went into the springhouse.

Em turned in and walked down the short lane to the yard gate. When the old lady came out of the springhouse, she was almost facing him. He took off his cap and greeted her respectfully. The gentle old woman looked him over searchingly, and instantly approved.

"Good morning. My name is Emerson Chadwick," he said. "I am on my way to the next town to see if I can get a job. My mother is dead, and I have no home. I will pull weeds or hoe, or even scrub floors. I am not afraid of work."

"Why, I don't believe you are!" she said in a high sweet voice. She unhooked the gate and held it open. "All my folks have had their breakfast and are gone to the fields. But you come in now, and I'll fix up a snack. You can work afterward. You look as skinny as a timber wolf."

Em laughed with her at this dry old simile and followed her into the kitchen. She shook her apron at the screen door briskly while they entered, so that no flies would come in.

She had him sit down at a little table covered with a crisp finen cloth and set an old blue plate, some silver, and a tall glass in front of him. Then she put some cobs in the fire to liven it up, shook down the ashes, and put a lump of butter in the frying pan to melt. In a few minutes Em was appreciatively eating fried eggs, stewed apples, honey, and homemade bread, topped by all the creamy milk he could drink. It was the best food he had ever eaten.

His courage rose as he ate.

When he had finished, she gave him a pair of overalls and let him change. "So you won't get those pretty pants dirty," she said.

He did a most thorough job of hoeing and weeding her garden. Before he left, she gave him a good filling dinner of mashed potatoes, gravy, cabbage slaw, roast, and pie. Then she directed him on his way.

*Now mind, if you don't find work, you come back here. Even if we can't pay you wages, we can let you do chores for your keep. I hate to see a young boy like you out alone against the world.*

"You just go a mile farther west till you come to the crossroads. Then turn south a mile and a quarter, and you'll come to Fabertown. It's one of the best little towns in southern Indiana. I'm sure you'll get a job there. My! I wish we needed a hand. I'd take you in a minute. But you be a good boy, Emerson. God bless you."

Thanking her courteously, Emerson started out toward Fabertown. As he was closing the gate, she called to him, "Now mind, if you don't find work, you come back here. Even if we can't pay you wages, we can let you do chores for your keep. I hate to see a young boy like you out alone against the world."

Emerson's heart warmed to her kindness. He thanked her and trudged on.

*The streets were full of horses and buggies and wagons.*

# Em Finds a Job

**H**EARTENED by the good breakfast and dinner and the kind words of the old lady, Em started at a brisk gait toward the little town. He had never felt so lighthearted in his life. True, he had not a penny in his pocket, but the call of a new and better life was infinite riches to him.

He was clean and neat, and his trousers and coat made him look much like any schoolboy of his age. That is how he wanted to look. All his schooldays he had had to endure jibes because of his rags and tatters. The boys of good birth and breeding simply didn't have anything to do with him, not because of what he was, but because of what he appeared to be. He would get a job now and forget all about the past.

While he was thus reflecting on the step he had taken, he rapidly covered the distance and Fabertown came into view. It was a busy little city, swarming with country trade. The stores were teeming little centers of prosperity, and the streets were full of horses and buggies and wagons. Em walked around the town a little to size it up. There were prosperous grocery stores, hardware stores with hog troughs and chicken brooders on display, and dry-goods stores with bolts of goods and models of ladies in dresses and coats with leg-o'-mutton sleeves in the window. The more he saw of it, the better it pleased him.

He went up one street and down another, watching for something, he knew not what. He wanted work, or a place of some kind for himself. He felt confident he would find it. Finally on a side street he saw a large brick building with the sign in front, "FABERTOWN WOOD PATTERN WORKS." From within he could hear the whine of the saws as they bit into the soft wood. The sound was a thrill to Em, for he had always wanted to work with his hands, but had had no chance to do so. He stood thinking, the noise of the machinery music to his ears. He finally went up to the door and looked in at the busy men and the saws. Some of the men were working with wood chisels, others with sandpaper. The floor was covered with curly shavings. The place smelled like a pine woods. Em loved it.

Then he noted a little office up front in a corner. It was not a real room—it was merely partitioned off by clean unpainted boards about waist high. A man was busy at a desk filing away some papers. Em approached him hesitantly but hopefully. The man looked up. Em saw that he was young and that his face was kind. He asked Em what he wanted in the same tone of voice he would have used with an adult.

"Wh-why," stammered the boy, actually nonplussed by the politeness, "I-I'd like to work here. I'd like to learn this trade. I'm all alone, and I've got to earn my own way. You don't have an opening for a boy, do you?" Em's eyes were filled with hope.

Quickly the man thought. There was an opening, he knew, but it was for a grown man. Would this young stripling do? Probably he could learn and learn fast, if he would. He had half a mind to try the young fellow out, and see what he was made of. He had the look of one who could be depended upon.

"Yes, I have an opening," he said aloud. "But, son, it's for a man. You don't think you could do a man's work, do you?"

He was trying the boy out. If this boy was a braggart, he wouldn't have him on the place for any money. He watched him closely as he waited for his answer.

Em flushed.

"Why, why, I haven't any experience," he replied sorrowfully, "but I'm willing to learn. I'd maybe make a lot of mistakes at first. I guess everyone does when they start, don't they? I need a job, Mister. I'll work—oh, I'll show you. I haven't a home—I have to work."

> *You'll do, son. I'll try you. You look as though you're made of good stuff.*

Em looked up shyly to see the gray eyes of the young man fastened on him.

"You'll do, son. I'll try you. You look as though you're made of good stuff. Now you say you haven't got a home. Where did you live? Where do you stay now? You say you have no folks. Surely you have someone."

"No," said the boy slowly. "I haven't got anyone. At least, anyone who cares for me. I did live in Dayton, but the people I stayed with— they— well, I left home. I came in here only this afternoon."

The young superintendent looked at him sternly, with sudden suspicion in his eyes.

"You haven't run away from home, have you, young fellow? Because if you have, you'll always regret it. And I can't hire you if you have left a good home just for a skylark. No good ever comes of things like that."

"Good home!" groaned Em bitterly. "Oh, Mister, if you could have seen it!" Then acting on an impulse, he told his new friend all about his little can of money; how he had intended to buy the newsstand, and his heartbreak and disappointment when he found that the money was gone; how he didn't have the courage to stay and try any longer when there was nothing to try for.

"In that case," said the young man sympathetically, "I shall help you. What's your name? Here, write it on this piece of paper. You are now one of our employees. Go get those overalls hanging on the wall over there. You can change in the washroom. You won't want to spoil that nice outfit. Then you can clean up the shavings under the machines. When the men call for boards or tools, take them to them. That will be your first job. My name is Sid Graham."

Em hurried away with a joyful heart to put on his working clothes. What did it matter if he didn't have a cent and didn't know where supper could come from? Something would happen. He wouldn't starve. He could maybe walk out and work for that old lady at the farm again evenings and mornings. No, he couldn't do that. He would be late for work. Oh, well, something would turn up. All through the long afternoon he worked busily at his task. The floor had never been cleaner, and all the men remarked about how nice and obliging the new boy was. They had taken an instant and warm liking to him, especially after Sid told them his story when he was out at the incinerator.

After quitting time Sid called Em to his desk. "What are you going to do till you get your first pay?" he asked. "I take it that you'll need a place to sleep and something to eat. Most of us do." He laughed a nice laugh, showing white, even teeth.

"Why, I haven't any plans," replied Em. "Lem got every cent of my money."

"Well, come with me, then, Emerson. I know of a good respectable boarding house where you can stay for a reasonable price. You won't have to pay in advance if I vouch for you."

The two started up the street. Em was very hungry, and his heart bounded ahead to the approaching reality of a clean bed, a neat table, a clean house. He wanted that more than anything.

Sid Graham vouched for him in the old-fashioned brick house, whose refined old mistress had had to take in boarders to stretch her slender income. She used her fragile old china and her thin solid silver and her linen tablecloths, ironed till they seemed to be glazed.

Em was assigned a beautiful big room on the third floor front, with a little round tower corner, where an old cherry desk was standing. Here he could sit and look far down the somber old street. The room was covered from wall to wall with carpet in a delightful old pattern of elaborate curlicues and intricate scrollwork. The bureau was wide and had a good mirror.

But the bed! Em approached it fearfully. Would it be like what he remembered beds ought to be? Clumsily he began his examination. Yes, here was the spread, white and smooth. Next a blanket, woolly and soft. Then —oh joy!—sheets, white as the driven snow. Two of them! The first one was tucked around the mattress, the second folded back over the blanket. Just as Mother Alice used to have it in those long-lost beautiful years! Big, plump pillows covered with snowy cases!

A silvery tinkle brought him up sharp. The supper bell!

He went over to the washstand, where a large china water pitcher presided over a huge washbowl. They were decorated with pretty gold and red carnations. The washstand was attractive with its stiffly starched splasher and its ample array of snowy towels and washcloths. A cake of lavender soap lay in a soap dish that matched the big pitcher and bowl. Em poured water into the bowl and washed up quickly. Then putting on his clean clothes and combing his black hair, he hurried down to supper.

The gentle old woman showed him his place at one end of the side of the long table. Candles were burning on the sideboard, and a curious Roman gold hanging lamp gave a soft, mellow glow to the room. He was introduced to all the other "guests," as the old lady called them. There was Miss Sessions, the dressmaker; Mrs. Tucker, a widow; and Mr. Harper. Then everyone wanted to know who he was and what he did. Em felt his heart swell with pride when he told the inquisitive little group that he had come from Dayton and was learning to be a patternmaker at the Fabertown Wood Pattern Works. A new era had begun for him.

# In With the Wrong Crowd

I T WOULD have been a wonderful thing if Emerson had made good friends in his new home. But Satan is ever awaiting his chance to make trouble. Before Em had been in Fabertown a year, he was running with a fast crowd. He learned to smoke, to play cards, and to play poker and pool. He steadfastly refused to drink—he had seen too much of the disgusting things Lem had done while drunk—but he often went to the theater. In fact, he took in everything sensational in Fabertown. And, as so often happens, punishment caught up with him sure and swift. The gang usually came calling for him right after supper.

"What's on tonight, fellows?" he would inquire casually.

"Oh, a game of poker at Bengy's. Come on." And the boys began giving him an education in the ways of evil that Em must entirely unlearn. He thought he was having a good time. Poor boy, he had never yet tasted God's pleasures, clean and satisfying. He had not known the "peace of God, which passeth all understanding."

*He thought he was having a good time. Poor boy, he had never yet tasted God's pleasures, clean and satisfying. He had not known the "peace of God, which passeth all understanding."*

Sometimes their pleasures took a vicious turn, as on the night they stole all the apples from a man's orchard and filled several gunny sacks with the fruit. Not satisfied with stealing, they broke the branches off and nearly ruined five beautiful trees. Finally, they placed the gunny sacks full of the apples on the back porches of the poorest homes in town. It was no help to the families who received them, however, for it got them in trouble with the police.

People began to complain about the gang. Things they had not done were laid at their door. Soon the police got on their trail.

Finally, their "fun" took a new turn. One of the boys noticed that a revival meeting was in progress south of the town. One of them proposed that they all go and "have some fun." They sallied forth one night, good-naturedly enough, but not realizing that they were a menace to the community.

The boys went out to the roughly built structure that had been rented to people of a certain religious group for the revival meeting. They crept up close to the windows, snickering and nudging one another, and peered in. The meeting was just getting under way. The preacher had worked himself up to a frenzy and had already taken off his coat and vest. The people were swaying back and forth, mumbling and moaning and shouting till the preacher had to shout to make himself heard. When the appeal came for them to come to the altar, the noise became deafening. Men and women leaped into the air. The whole congregation surged forward.

The crowd of boys at the window decided on action. Of course they meant it only in fun, but the volley of big, soft mud balls they hurled landed with soft splats right in the midst of the hysterical crowd and well-nigh broke up the meeting. Jake was such a good shot that he got the preacher squarely in the mouth. People who were supposed to be speaking in unknown tongues began to yell in irate English over the sudden deluge of mud. The boys stopped long enough to bend over with convulsive laughter at the spectacle, but when alert to their danger, they took to their heels as one man. A few men from the congregation gave chase, but by dodging this way and that the group finally got together in a favorite rendezvous in a fishing shack by the river and decided they had had a capital good time.

"Wasn't that funny! Oh, boy! Ha! Ha! Ho! Ho! I can see that preacher still spluttering!" And Hank lay down on the floor of the old shed and rolled with mirth.

"Lay low, fellows! I hear someone," cautioned Em, who was keeping guard. "Sh-sh-sh."

The boys heard the crackle of the grass outside. In some unknown way their pursuers had got on their track. Silence reigned in the old shanty. Then shuffling toward the door, the boys by common consent crept outside. Not far away they could see bobbing lanterns.

"Come on, fellows. Run for it!" hissed Jake. And crouching low, they crept as noiselessly as they could along the crackling willow branches lining the riverbank toward the dim outline of the bridge. Looking back, they saw that the bobbing lanterns had drawn nearer and had entered the fishing shack.

"Fellows, we'd have been caught sure if we had stayed there," breathed Jim Hardy, the daredevil of the group.

They thought all along that their pursuers were merely outraged members of the meeting they had just broken up. But the bobbing lanterns revealed the fact that they were policemen. The boys could see the brass

*"Lay low, fellows. I hear someone," cautioned Em.*

buttons on their chests glow in the light of the lanterns. They were scared out of their wits. Now they could hear a word or two of the policemen's conversation.

"—been a regular run of hoodlums in the town."

"—won't rest till we get those smart alecks shut up."

"The town will be glad to be shut of them."

The boys were now thoroughly frightened and turned almost white with fear. Quaking, they crept across the bridge and ran like fleet deer across fields and over hills for the village.

Just on the edge of the town they came upon a large vacant lot near the city park.

"What's that?" Hank voiced the silent inquiry of the whole bunch of them when a big tent, its sides aglow with light, came into view. "A circus, I bet you!" he whispered. "Let's get in."

They crept around the big tent, lighted by hissing gas flares, till they came to a darker part. Then all four boys wriggled under.

But it was not a show. It was a religious meeting. Em in particular was struck with the fact that it was different from the meeting they had just left. The audience sat silently and respectfully listening to the preacher. The speaker was saying things, not merely shouting to work up hysteria. There was an air of sanctity about the place that had been wholly missing in the other meeting.

Then Em noted several charts made out of canvas hanging on the tent wall. At one side was the picture of a tall image. It had been painted in a strange way. The head was gold, the chest, silver. Beside it were pictures of beasts—beasts like, yet unlike, some he had seen in parades. They were the queerest looking things!

But the preacher was referring to the chart. Pointing to it, he repeated a Bible text: "In the days of these kings shall the God of heaven set up a kingdom, which shall never be—"

But, interested as Em was, he did not get to hear the rest. A heavy hand was laid on his shoulder. He looked up fearfully into the face of a big policeman.

His heart plunged with fear. He looked wildly about for a way to escape, but the boys were all caught and were swiftly piloted out of the tent. The other boys were begging like good fellows to be released. A moment before they had been swaggeringly brave, but now, cheeks pale, lips blue, they were crying for mercy.

"Aw, come on. Let us off. We didn't do anything. My dad will lick the tar out of me if I get into trouble."

Jake was the most venturesome boy of all in their depredations, but he was frankly blubbering and squirming in the firm grasp of his captor.

"You fellows have been regular pests all over this town, with your thieving and your meddling," replied the big blue guardian of the law. "I am going to lock you up and let you cool your heels in jail. Breaking up two meetings in one evening! Didn't you know you'd catch it, sooner or later? I'm surprised at you!"

Em replied indignantly at this. "Only one, Mister!" he protested. "We didn't break up this last one. I wouldn't have wanted to, either. I wish I could have stayed and heard what the preacher had to say. It sounded interesting, with those pictures and charts. I wish I knew what they meant."

"A likely story," sneered the policeman. "A fellow that breaks up one meeting will more than likely break up two."

And the boys, scared as rabbits, were hustled into a black patrol wagon and rushed off to jail.

That first night in prison was agony for Emerson. He didn't sleep a wink all night. Guilt and humiliation ground into his very soul. He knew he had done wrong. He deserved what he was getting. He wanted someone—oh, someone! What he needed, though he did not know, and would have vigorously denied it if he had been told, was Jesus Christ to come in and give him a new heart.

In the morning Sid, his employer, came and gave him a good talking to. "Now listen, boy," he said kindly, "I don't want you to get mixed up with that lazy, good-for-nothing gang anymore. They are a menace to the town, and everyone is against them. You mark my word, every one of those boys will yet see the inside of a penitentiary if he doesn't straighten up. And you will, too, Emerson, if you run with them."

The boy later saw this prophecy fulfilled to the letter in the lives of the other boys.

Emerson sat dejectedly on his narrow cot, cut to the soul. He had drifted along with the gang, entering into their fun, smoking with them, playing cards with them, and accompanying them on their tours of thievery and destruction. He had learned bad words from them, and now his conversation included slang, coarse and obscene, and profanity of the baser sort. He was a different boy entirely from what he had been more than a year before when he had left Dayton, penniless and brokenhearted.

After Sid left, Em walked up and down in his narrow cell to while away the dragging hours. "Whatever got into me is more than I can figure out!" he would mumble a dozen times a day. Then he thought back on the uselessness of his life.

While he sat there and sweated and worried in his enforced idleness, the Wright brothers were packing their machinery and gliders snugly into their hangar at Kitty Hawk, preparatory to going back to Dayton. They had built a fine glider entirely on their own calculations. Em had read of it in the paper. And that summer it had been flown successfully many times. They had at last gotten it to fly a distance of 622 feet. And here was he, Emerson Chadwick, in jail at a time when the world was teetering on the brink of amazing new things!

Because this was his first arrest, Emerson was soon released. The next four years were uneventful. He didn't do much except work hard at his job, go home, eat, sleep, and work hard at his job again. He became honest and respectable, but not in the least religious. The only real interest he had ever taken in religion was that night in the tent. But when he got out of jail and went to look for the tent, it was gone, no one knew where. His zest for saving money had again asserted itself, and he added steadily, week by week, to his account at the local bank.

He had grown into a singularly handsome man, too. He had his mother's black hair and dark brown eyes. He had his father's height and clear, fair complexion.

But two great changes were in store for Emerson, and one was not far off.

# Great Changes

ONE DAY something happened that was to change Emerson's whole life. He was in his early twenties, sober and full of business, when he saw a girl. He was swinging down Main Street looking neither to the right nor to the left, when he saw her. She was looking at a display of fall dresses in a variety store window. Stopping at the window of a store next to it, Emerson pretended to be interested in the piles of clothespins, pie tins, and eggbeaters in the window—as if a young man his age would be interested in such things! Really, he was looking at the girl out of the corner of his eye.

Suddenly he realized that she looked somewhat like his mother! His lost, precious mother! Her face was pretty and gentle, yet she looked capable and practical, too.

It was perhaps a silly thing to do, but he loitered around town at a discreet distance and watched her. He forgot whatever errand it was he had been in such a hurry about a little earlier. At last, when she went home, he followed afar off and found out where she lived. Now to meet her! How would he go about it?

At last, in a social gathering, they were introduced. Her character was as lovely as she had appeared to him at first. She was dainty, neat, and modest, with a keen, alert mind. It seemed almost too good to be true. Hence at the age of twenty-one Emerson found himself in love with beautiful Mary Winton. Her parents liked him, too, for he was respected all over the town. He began to keep regular company with her, and went to her home frequently.

"Come in! Come in!" Pa Winton opened the door for him one evening. "Come in here and sit for a while. Mary's not ready yet anyhow. Beats all how girls and women can fritter away time with their frills and laces and gewgaws. But laying all other matters aside, Emerson, did you see that horseless carriage that went through town today? That snorting thing surely scared the horses. My horse dragged the hitch weight clear down Sycamore Street and nearly turned the surrey over. When I finally caught up with him, he was like a wild horse, rearing and plunging and his eyes rolling. I tell you, there ought to be a law—"

"Oh, but Mr. Winton!" interrupted Em, his eyes shining. "Horseless carriages are the coming thing! Why, I believe that before long you'll have to comb the city to find horses. These horseless carriages will be perfected year by year till—"

A loud roar of laughter greeted Emerson's eager predictions.

"Visionary! Visionary! Emerson! Why those things will never be used by anybody but the riffraff. Now take the womenfolk. They were never made to understand machinery; their heads aren't capable of it. But every woman who has a grain of sense can handle a good, gentle horse. No, Emerson, don't let your head get full of wild schemes like that. Just let a few of those noisy carriages get loose and run wild, or catch fire and explode, and we'll have this gas-buggy notion out of people's heads and have some peace and quiet again. Well, here's Mary. Where are you going this evening?"

"Over to Sophie's. She's giving a party," said Mary, and they were gone.

Theirs was a wonderful friendship. Mary insisted that they attend church regularly, and Emerson entered joyfully into this new phase of his life. He began to look at life a little differently. One could not live for self alone, he realized. He began to feel his need of God.

He worked harder than ever, and was even more careful and meticulous about his clothes and his person. He was more anxious than ever to save his money. He tried harder to be good. He wanted more than anything in life to be worthy of her.

Evidently Mary felt the same toward him, for one evening when he stammered out a proposal, she graciously accepted.

They picked out their little house and purchased it before the wedding. Emerson would have nothing else. He wanted to have a pretty place to which to take her immediately. For several weeks the two of them had scoured Fabertown hunting for just the right house. They had eventually found exactly what they wanted. It was down a quiet, sleepy street and was built of brick, with deep, cool porches mantled with lush ivy.

When the young people were going through the house, Granny Cutlip, who owned the place, ventured a suggestion: "Now, children, why don't you buy it just as it stands? I want to get rid of my things; you want to buy things. I've always bought the best and taken good care of it. You can have it for—," and she named a figure for the little house and its furniture that almost took Em's and Mary's breath away, it was so reasonable. The two looked at each other in amazement.

They both knew that if they bought new things they could never be so massive and lovely as Granny's beautiful old mahogany and early American treasures.

"They've been in the family for years and years," lamented the old lady with a grain of mournful pride in her voice. "But, oh my! Children nowadays turn up their noses at old stuff. The new stuff can't hold a candle to this old mahogany. But what do I care? I'll soon be dead and gone. Now if you'll take the stuff as it is, I'll throw in my set of Haviland china. One-hundred-piece set it is, and I've never so much as broken a teacup."

They bought it, of course, and Granny moved out immediately.

The day of their wedding was crisp and cold. The air was bracing, and then in the afternoon snow began to fall. It was a day they would cherish all their fives.

After they had lived in their little home about a month, Mary told Emerson one evening that she had had callers. Her eyes were shining.

"Oh, Em, it was a neighbor woman. She lives right next door there to the south in that big, comfortable two-story house. Well, she and her eldest son were here. I never talked to a woman like her!"

"What is her name?" inquired Em, interested at once.

They were lingering over supper in the kitchen. The table had been set near the western window, and the firelight glowed with a toothy red grin from the shining cookstove. The teakettle began its bubbly song, then ran over, and the drops chased one another all over the stove lid, till they had hissingly done away with themselves.

"Her name is McRae," answered his wife, as she gathered up the cups. "We got to talking about gas buggies and airships, and she said that it's written in the Bible, plain as day, that in the 'last days' 'knowledge shall be increased' and 'many shall run to and fro.' She says she believes that gas buggies and airships and printing presses are all signs that the world is corning to an end."

There arose briefly in Em's mind a little scene he had hung far back on the walls of memory. A chart, strange and interesting, of queer beasts and a great image. That one sentence he had heard the preacher say came to him again. "In the days of these kings shall the God of heaven set up a kingdom, which shall never be destroyed." Why, he must have been preaching the coming of the Lord, too.

"Even that boy, too—he must be about fourteen or fifteen—" resumed Mary, "just sat here and talked as clever and smart as a teacher—or a preacher either, for that matter." Mary was washing the dishes now, her rosy arms plunged deep into sudsy water. The silver was carefully washed and rinsed, then the glassware, while the cups were soaking. After she had washed out her dish towels and hung them on a little line on the back porch, they left the kitchen in perfect order and went to the parlor.

"Once," reminisced Em, when he had settled himself in the Sleepy Hollow rocker near the big lamp, "once when I was a boy here in town, right after I got here from Dayton, I heard a fragment of a sermon about the last days. Well, it was hardly a fragment. It was only one sentence. It was that night the East End gang and I were arrested for breaking up that meeting. We came sneaking into town, hiding from the police, and we thought the big tent we saw when we got into town was a show tent, and crawled under. But it wasn't. It was a religious meeting. The man had big charts up in front, with pictures on them, and was pointing to the toes of an image and reading a verse from somewhere in the Bible. I will never forget that verse. It was, 'In the days of these kings shall the God of heaven set up a kingdom, which shall never be destroyed.' Just then the police caught up, and I didn't hear any more of the sermon."

"But didn't you go back afterward and find out?" inquired Mary.

"Yes, I did," answered Em, "but the tent was gone. I don't know of anything religious that stirred me the way that one sentence did."

"I'll ask Mrs. McRae sometime if she ever heard of that verse. Maybe she can find it. She surely knows a lot of Bible."

"Oh, no, don't bother, Mary. They'll think we're silly, asking them questions like that. Of course she wouldn't know. The Bible is a terribly big Book. I believe that preacher knew his business. I have a feeling that if I could find one like him, he could really tell me something."

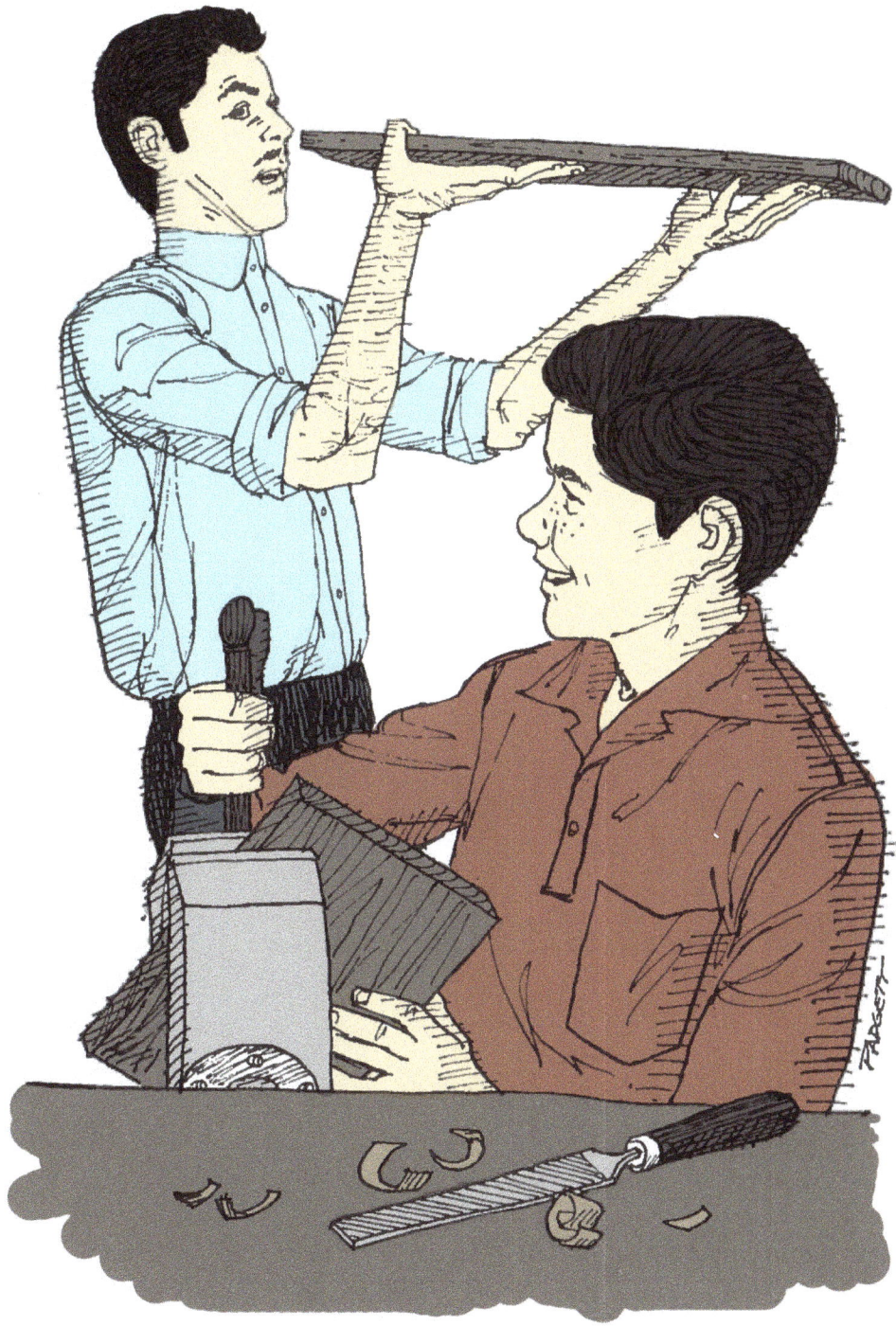

*Calvin loved to help Emerson make beautiful things in his workshop.*

# Sickness in the Night

A LITTLE brick building that used to be a milkhouse stood in the back yard of the Chadwick home. Emerson fitted it up into a workshop. Along one side he built benches. Overhead were shelves for tools and drawers for screws and nails. He made Mary a beautiful cedar chest bound with brass bands, and corner cupboards for the kitchen.

Calvin, the boy next door, soon took to coming in and helping him, showing a real interest in all that was going on.

"What can I do, Mr. Chadwick?" he would ask wistfully, as he watched the clean shavings curl up and overflow the smoothing plane. He was itching to get his hands on the smooth boards and help.

"Well, you can take these legs and rub them with sandpaper. Then I'll chisel out the grooves for mortising. It will take a lot of work to get this chair done, but I'm going to have it finished by Mary's birthday next week."

The two of them grew to be great friends, and every spare moment Calvin was over across the yards in the little shop with Em.

"Come over tomorrow, and we'll start to make a whatnot for your mom," offered Em one Friday afternoon when he met the boy as he was going home from work. "I've got some pretty cherry wood."

The lad was watching the sun anxiously as he hurried along with his arms full of packages from the grocery store. He stopped for a minute, the rays of the waning sun full on his eager face. He laughed a little as he shook his thick black hair. "Why, Mr. Chadwick," he asked, "didn't you know we are Seventh-day Adventists and keep the seventh-day Sabbath? We always go to church on Saturday and keep it as our rest day."

Em stopped and looked the lad full in the face, disbelief written all over his features. "You keep Saturday!" he exclaimed. "How come you do that? Are you Jews? I never heard of anyone except Jews going to church on Saturday!"

"*We* do, Mr. Chadwick, and we are not Jews. But the Bible says that that is the day to keep. There's not a text in all the Bible that gives anybody permission to keep another day. I must hurry home now. I have some things I must get done before sundown. You see, we keep the Sabbath from sundown to sundown, and mom always says we must guard the edges of the Sabbath." He waved his hand at Em and swung off at an easy gait up the street.

"All boy, every inch of him," thought Em, as he gazed at his retreating figure. "A shame, though, for his family to be fanatical over religion that way." He proceeded slowly home, turning the whole thing over in his mind.

Soon new joy was added to Em's life. A lovely baby girl, whom they named Alice, filled their lives with fresh happiness. Their evenings were different now. More than likely Mary had the sewing table out, and her scissors would be clipping gently through fine dimities and other pretty fabrics for baby.

There was something satisfying about reading the evening paper with the gentle mother stroking ruffles with a needle, and baby Alice between them saying "A-goo, a-goo!" conversationally to whichever one happened to notice her.

Sometimes Em took her up, and she would laugh and coo and make herself so adorable that he wondered how he had ever been happy in life without her.

When evening came, she was eager for her daddy to come home. She seemed to sense when it was time, and her little fat face would be peering eagerly through the bars of the crib at him when he came through the door.

Em was conscious one night, late in the winter, that Mary was up with the baby. She was careful not to disturb him when little Alice was cross. He heard her open up the drafts of the heater and fill the teakettle. Then he must have dozed off again, for he was suddenly awakened by Mary shaking him. He almost perished with fright when he saw that she was crying. Her face was drawn and pale, and in the lamplight her lips were blue.

"Em! Em! Get up quickly and go for the doctor! It's Alice, Em! I think she's dying!"

Em was out of bed in an instant and beside the crib. The baby's eyes had rolled back, and the noise of her breathing, loud and laborious, filled the room.

"What's the matter with her, Mary?" Emerson asked, lips stiff and eyes dilated with fear.

"I don't know, but I'm afraid it's croup. Run over to the fire station and phone Dr. Lunston —and hurry! Hurry, Em! See how hard it is for her to breathe."

Em was flinging on his clothes. His fingers were all thumbs. Mary was bathing Alice's hot head and neck with a washcloth wrung out of warm water.

Em raced for the telephone. On the way back, on an impulse, he ran up and knocked on Mrs. McRae's door. She was a good neighbor and mother. Maybe she could help Mary till the doctor came. He tried to still his thumping heart while he knocked. To be without Alice—oh, what would life be without her? What could he do without her?

The door opened, and motherly Mrs. McRae stood before him. In a few broken words he told her what had happened.

"Of course," she said simply, "I'll be there right away!"

It seemed that he had hardly got back to the bedroom before Mrs. McRae came in quietly and took charge of things.

"It is croup," she said. "I know it is. My Calvin had it often when he was young."

With skilled fingers she began making a tent of some large woolen cloths. Then Calvin entered, carrying a kerosene heater. Mrs. McRae lighted it deftly and set the boiling teakettle on it in such a way that the steam entered the little tent where baby Alice was struggling for her life.

Mary stood back in amazement, dumbly obeying orders for towels, washcloths, and cool water. By the time the doctor came, the baby was breathing easier. He gazed at the tent in approval. And when he had looked at the baby and found out how long they had been working over her, he shook his head.

"I'll tell you frankly, Mr. Chadwick, Mrs. McRae has saved your baby. I came as fast as I could, but I was out working over Mr. Bender. He had another heart attack. If you had done nothing till I came, it would have been—well, too late. You can just thank your lucky stars for a neighbor like her!"

Mrs. McRae flushed warmly over the praise, but she worked on, till little Alice was breathing naturally. The sky was streaked with day when she started for home. Her face was sagging with weariness, but she smiled at Em's and Mary's eager thanks and refused to take any pay for her help.

"Now you tell us, Mrs. McRae," urged the young man, "whenever we can do anything for you! Why, words are futile. There's no way we can ever tell you how we appreciate it. Call on us when you need us, won't you?"

"Oh, I will," she replied, smiling wearily.

But she little realized how soon and how terrible that summons would be.

# Faith Takes Wings

CALVIN McRAE came over nearly every day to play with Alice. She grew to know him and would shout, "Cow, Cow!" in an effort to say Calvin, when she saw him coming. Sometimes he would get down her blocks and build towers for her. She would wait with infinite patience, her blue eyes sparkling, till he got them built teeteringly high, then she would spat them with her pink palm and shout, "Bwake!" And the boy's deep chuckle and Alice's high trebly one would join in happy laughter as the tower fell down and the blocks were scattered all over the floor.

"I tell you," Em would often comment to Mary, "it's out of the ordinary for a big fellow like that to be so gentle with a baby."

"You're right," responded his wife in a whisper. "Isn't it a shame his folks have that funny religion? It practically ostracizes him from the rest of the boys! You never see him with any of the young fellows his own age!"

"Well, I don't know that that hurts him any," mused Em. "The only time I ever ran with a gang I got into all kinds of trouble. No, Mary, religion or no religion, I wouldn't want Calvin to change a whit. He's just as near perfect as any boy I ever saw."

One day Emerson and the lad got to talking about airplanes, and Emerson was astonished to learn that Calvin knew all about them. Just to test him, he pretended to be skeptical.

"They may be all right for stunts and fairs, Calvin, but for actual use in business—why, I don't believe they'll ever be very useful." He waited for the boy's reaction.

"Oh, but they're doing it now! There are lots of people working on airships these days! Why, they'll be thicker than flies!" Then the boy straightened up and looked Em in the eye. "Know why I believe it, Mr. Chadwick?" he asked soberly. "Because it says in the Bible, over in Daniel, that in the time of the end 'many shall run to and fro, and knowledge shall be increased.' Why, I remember when I was a little boy, people were scared of automobiles. Used to call them horseless carriages and gas buggies. All the old-timers used to say that nobody but daredevils and the riffraff would ever have them. Now look, Mr. Chadwick! Several people have them right here in Fabertown. Lawyer Blanchard bought one, an Apperson. Is it ever a beaut! And Dr. Byron Smith has a Haynes."

"Why is it, Calvin," Emerson asked him suddenly, later that evening, "that I never see you running around with any of the boys of the neighborhood? You seem to lead a lonely life. I would think you'd like to have a chum or a pal of some kind."

Calvin's face was sober. He looked down for a while, then up and into Em's eyes. "Well, you see, Mr. Chadwick, it's like this. My religion is, well, different. I can't, and I won't, do things the other boys do when they're running around. I don't believe it is right. You know old Apple Mary, the lady who sells apples on a cart on Maple Street? Well, there have been some fellows making her life miserable lately. They upset her cart today, and I helped her set it up and pick up the apples. Then someone reported the boys, and the police arrested them. They warned them that they would really be in for trouble if anything like this happened again. Now they think I told the police.

"On my way here tonight, Hodge Phillips stopped me outside your gate. I could tell he was angry, and he said, 'The boys are out to get you.' Mr. Chadwick, I don't know whether they will carry out their threat or not, but I can't join that gang. It would break mother's heart for me to get mixed up with a rough bunch like that. She wants me to be a Christian— not a hoodlum."

"But, Calvin, I would think you would be frightened, having a threat like that hanging over you," exclaimed Emerson.

"It's not too pleasant," Calvin replied, "but I am sure God will let nothing happen to me that is not for the best. If He lets me get shot, good will come of it, I know."

A few minutes later he got up to leave. "Come back soon," Emerson called after him. Calvin waved from the gate, and Emerson closed the door and turned to pick up Alice.

Scarcely had he set her on his knee when he and Mary heard a shot in the quiet street. Then such shouting and disorder arose that Emerson ran outside to see what had happened. Already a crowd had gathered.

"What's the trouble?" he asked a bystander.

"Someone got shot," the man answered.

Fear gripped Emerson's heart. Had the gang carried out their threat so soon?

"Do you know who it was?"

"No. They think it was some young fellow who lived on this street."

Emerson pushed his way through the crowd. He had to find out who was hurt, though he dreaded what he might discover. And then he saw him—Calvin, dead, killed by a young gangster crazy for revenge.

It became Emerson's terrible duty to tell the mother.

" 'The Lord gave, and the Lord hath taken away,' " she said, and fainted outright.

The newspapers were full of the story next day. And when Emerson told the police about the man who had threatened Calvin, they really got busy.

When the day of the funeral arrived, the streets near the McRae house were filled with carriages, buggies, and cabs. Emerson rented a buggy for himself and Mary so that they could go to the cemetery.

When they entered the crowded little church and chose seats as near the front as possible, Emerson's eyes were drawn to large charts tacked on the wall near the pulpit. They were strangely familiar. At one side was the picture of a great image. There were pictures of beasts of several kinds, too—queer beasts with many horns, and some that even had wings. They were charts exactly like the ones he had seen in the tent so long, long ago. Now he was back to the very place where he knew he could find truth. And Calvin—gentle, good Calvin—had led him here, though he never knew it.

After the service, when everyone else had left, Emerson had a long talk with the pastor of that little Seventh-day Adventist church. "Calvin had something in his life I wish I had in mine," he confessed to the preacher. "He was so, well, so kind and patient."

The pastor smiled in a friendly way. "I think the difference was," he said, "that Calvin knew the Master, and you have not become acquainted with Him yet."

"You're right," Emerson admitted. "But how can I learn about Him?"

"I'll be glad to come over to your house and study the Bible with you," the minister offered.

And so it was arranged—the day Calvin was buried. For weeks the studies went on, and at last Emerson and Mary were baptized and took little Alice with them to Sabbath School.

From then on Emerson lived for the Lord, helping to win souls. Remembering what Gus had taught him about lettering, he made many a sign and diagram for evangelists to use to make their sermons more interesting and easier to understand.

He learned, too, to trust in the wings of faith, which would lift him up to the beauty of everlasting life. It had been wings, wings, wings, that

*Calvin was dead—killed by a young gangster crazy for revenge.*

had called him all his life. First, airship wings, helicopter wings. Then he had tried his own wings, and had fallen down, down, down, with that gang. Then Christ had come to him with healing in His wings. Yes, he, Emerson Chadwick, had traveled a long, hard way, and could trace the goodness and the graciousness of God in His untiring effort to build for him a good and respectable life, with a happy Christian home and a loving wife and family.

*** 

Now twenty-five years had passed since that day the shot was fired. Emerson, still kneeling by the headstone that marked Calvin's grave, sighed. He let the five-fingered ivy leaves slip from his fingers and fall back over the little marker, then stood stiffly to his feet.

"Thank you, Calvin," he murmured. "You did more for me than you ever realized. And thank You, God, too," he prayed reverently, "for bringing him into my life."

Suddenly he remembered that Mary was waiting for him in the car. And he hurried to her, for he knew she would be wondering why he had been so long at the grave.

**TEACH Services, Inc.**

P U B L I S H I N G

We invite you to view the complete
selection of titles we publish at:
**www.TEACHServices.com**

We encourage you to write us
with your thoughts about this,
or any other book we publish at:
**info@TEACHServices.com**

TEACH Services' titles may be purchased in
bulk quantities for educational, fund-raising,
business, or promotional use.
**bulksales@TEACHServices.com**

Finally, if you are interested in seeing
your own book in print, please contact us at:
**publishing@TEACHServices.com**
We are happy to review your manuscript at no charge.

www.ingramcontent.com/pod-product-compliance
Lightning Source LLC
Chambersburg PA
CBHW060444090426
42733CB00011B/2375